She Chased The World

The tragedies of trauma

Papikins

Cyrus Ahmadnia

Papikins

She chased the world

Copyright © 2021 by Cyrus Ahmadnia (Papikins)

All rights reserved. No part of this book may be reproduced in any form or by any electronic or mechanical means, including information storage and retrieval systems, without permission in writing from the publisher, except by a reviewer who may quote brief passages in a review.

This book is a creative work of poetic prose, which has been derived from various experiences and observations. However, some instances have been created from the imagination.

ISBN 978-1-9168832-2-2 (Paperback)

ISBN 978-1-9168832-3-9 (eBook)

Published by Papikins Publishing

www.papikins.com

Artist

Piyapong Saydaung

www.instagram.com/saydung.89

Papikins

She chased the world

This is dedicated to those who chase the world unwillingly. I'm sorry.

Papikins

Table of contents

Chase the world	1
Rose full of thorns	2
Beautiful disaster	3
Turned to stone	4
Into the blue	5
Smiling at catastrophe	6
Sadness behind her eyes	7
Perfect person	8
Conflicted	9
Picturesque	10
Starry skies	11
Showing teeth	12
Imperfect	13
Destruction	14
Keeping distance	15
Distractions	16
Trust	17
Vibrant yet chaotic	18
Demons	19
To be real	20

She chased the world

Selfish	21
Betrayed by blood	22
Fragile eyes	23
Scars	24
Broken heart	25
Venom and regret	26
Behind the mask	27
Fairy tales	28
She held the universe	29
The cycle	30
The wolves	31
A touch of sadness	32
Wronged	33
Afterthought	34
Fallen angel	35
Hurts like hell	36
Predator in disguise	37
Keeping quiet	40
Ruined	41
Somewhere to belong	42
The sun and the moon	43
Death	44

She chased the world

Empty space	45
Staring into heaven	46
Ghosts	47
Left the world	48
Sanity	49
Always ticking	50
Meaningless desires	51
Snakes	52
Friendship	53
Surrounded by lies	54
Nothing in return	55
Two-faced	56
Prying eyes	57
Damaged	58
The silence	59
The thinning crowd	60
The unheard	61
The beginning of the end	62
Self-belief	63
Revisiting the past	64
Someone else's sin	65
Voiceless	66

She chased the world

Ripped apart by wolves	67
A place within the world	68
Defenceless	69
Helpless	70
Validation	71
Another body	72
What once was	73
Break	74
Weightless wings	75
Painted smile	76
Intertwine	77
He gave her hope	78
Stories of a life once lived	79
Building trust	80
Fight through storms	81
Safe	82
Stories in her head	83
City lights	84
Just a dream	85
Part of sadness	86
The dates of surrender	87
Trapped	88

She chased the world

Loss of love	89
Cold embrace	90
Obscurity	91
Falling out of love	92
Neglected	93
'I love you'	94
Grown apart	95
The death of love	96
Someone else	97
Betrayal	98
Hiding deceit	99
Wolves among us	100
Another story	101
Back to loneliness	102
Keeping love alive	103
Repairing what love did	104
Only one in colour	105
Disposable	106
Tears full of memories	107
Beautiful yet flawed	108
Life of misery	109
Surrender to the night	110

She chased the world

A life to take	111
Spiral into madness	112
The canvas of life	113
One to blame	114
Goodbye and a simple lullaby	115
Running through time	116
Guilty	117
Vacant	118
Dreams	119
Losing strength	120
Misdirection	121
Paralysed	122
Beyond the scars	123
Fade	124
Drowning	125
Time	126
Short of breath	127
Normality	128
The last goodbye	129
The end of what she knew	130

Papikins

Chase the world

We try to chase the world. It isn't our intention to stay seated in one place, but it all becomes the same. It's the tragedies of trauma that make us feel a certain way. We're struck by disaster and our minds begin to fade. We fear for the worst to happen, but sometimes, we forget that life is made of pain. It's a sad realisation that none of us can ever come to terms with. We fight the tears every single day, but the ache never goes away. It's humanity, isn't it? We're individually flawed beyond what words can say. I just wish I didn't have to be the one to remind you of the reasons why we break.

This is the story of the girl who chased the world. She was a beautiful disaster through and through, and oh my god, she had emotions that no one dared to ever feel. She wanted to be real but was never satisfied with the cards that she'd been dealt. She was beautifully designed yet a tragedy that no one ever questioned. She would endlessly try to keep up with a world that moved without her. She was somewhere in the past, forgetting time was made to be a killer.

She chased the world

Rose full of thorns

She was a rose full of thorns and her problems were too heavy for her to hold, as she tried to chase the world. She could never stop for comfort because she felt so far behind. It's what happens when we rarely feel alive. We barely move with life, and it stops us from being present. She was caught up with indecision. It was her smile. It was always her smile. It would never stay consistent. It would conceal the thorns around her, as she tried to be as vibrant as a rose without composure. It was saddening to see her. She had an endearing demeanour, but truth be told, she would crumble at the slightest hint of failure.

She chased the world

Beautiful disaster

She was a beautiful disaster made from the hell that she encountered. Her eyes would sparkle under moonlight, as if they told a thousand stories that were only meant for night. They were the epitome of sincerity, yet shrouded by her insecurities. She hid beneath a smile which was infected by her tragedies. She would watch the rising sun, hoping to find herself within its light, but sadly, she never could. She never felt like she was enough to make her dreams come true.

She chased the world

Turned to stone

She held a weary smile as she travelled from place to place. She had always been accustomed to the taste of bittersweet pretence. Nothing could be real when she was fighting with regret. She would try to be somebody else, but ultimately lost herself instead. She found it hard to grow, because she was reminded of a heart that turned to stone. It was never her intention to fall without a reason, but as her life unfolded, she was forced into submission. She felt fragile and neglected, and that's what made her distant.

She chased the world

Into the blue

She fell into the blue, as if to say goodbye to what she knew. She had no recollection of who she was before she stumbled. It took away the memories she adored. She was on a search for happiness after losing all her innocence. It was never easy to find herself beyond the scars that left her vulnerable. She would try to find her happiness in the form of other people, yet little did she know, they would add on to her hell.

She chased the world

Smiling at catastrophe

There was an emptiness inside her, and it always seemed to lead to grief. She thought about her flaws as the silence crept into her head. She knew she was only made for tears but tried to smile at catastrophe instead. She would attach herself to moments, but they only made her worse. She wanted to be real in a place where poseurs ruled the world.

She chased the world

Sadness behind her eyes

She never seemed to fit within the life that she had wanted. She was frightened of the words that she kept in. She knew she risked exposure to the truths she felt within. The sadness behind her eyes was always kept a secret, as she tried her best to hide within the confines of regret. She was tired of the silence. She was tired of staring into nothing, as her heart was slowly breaking.

She chased the world

Perfect person

There were days where she would crumble, as heartbreak settled in. She surrendered to the thoughts of who she was and where she's been. She couldn't be a perfect person or anywhere in between. She was striving to succeed, but never saw herself as worthy. She needed to build her self-belief, but found it hard to breathe when her family disapproved of how she lived. They never allowed her to be the person she was crying out to be, as they tried to control her destiny.

Conflicted

She was conflicted by her soul and by her mind. They steered in opposite directions, as she coasted through her life. She was lost inside a world which never gave her hope. She wanted to find peace, but nothing helped to numb the quietness of being. She was led towards dishonesty and betrayal, but what hurt the most, is that her life had been derailed. There were demons and there were ghosts. They tore into her skin just to save themselves.

She chased the world

Picturesque

She would tear herself apart because she feared to be alive. She had a thousand thoughts inside her mind, but she failed to see that they were lies. She would hurt herself the most whenever she'd be left alone. She never had control over what her mind would say. It would only cause her to disconnect like a painting from its frame. She was picturesque and lovely, but sometimes beauty hides the imperfections of the soul. It was hard to see her clearly, especially when she always chased the world.

She chased the world

Starry skies

She stared outside her window each and every night, gazing up towards the starry skies. She had always been attracted to the stars and how they shined. She wished to be among them, as she followed the world from far behind. She wanted to be free, but never felt like she could fly. She never understood her wings were only meant to glide. She would only focus on the darkest side of life, as she compared herself to stars because they would only fade with time.

She chased the world

Showing teeth

She would hope for reasons to genuinely smile, but with all that she had been through, her lips were slightly stained with insincerity. They never truly functioned, or at least that's what she perceived. Those around her expected smiles from every corner, but instead, she'd only show them teeth. It was a part of her design that pushed her to the brink, as she tried her best to somehow find relief.

She chased the world

Imperfect

She would stare into the void, as she thought of ways to soften her mistakes. She would call herself imperfect, but deep down, she wanted to be closer to perfection. She never could admit it, but she was chasing something non-existent. She wanted to feel differently, but all she ever did was lose herself entirely.

She chased the world

Destruction

She would build her walls to break, as if her heart was stuck inside a cage. She was scared to leave herself defenceless, because she knew the outcomes before they had a chance to be presented. She had felt connection and resentment, and both were part of her destruction.

She chased the world

Keeping distance

She was always searching for someone to connect to, but after all the pain of trust, her fear of being open prevented her from getting close again. She would keep her distance from those who showed her interest, because she knew that she would lose them. She was familiar with seclusion, and she was too tired to feed her soul with loss.

She chased the world

Distractions

She would adapt to those around her, never showing her true self. She was scared that someone would ask her questions. They were too difficult to answer when her life was created from disaster. She held her story in, as she sat there with her friends. Her mind would always wonder – were they really friends, or passers-by who distracted her from life?

Trust

Trust is hard to come by. We let ourselves be immersed with ideas of sharing who we are, but we're burnt down time and time again. We can never truly trust anyone when we can barely trust ourselves. It's a sad realisation. There is no measuring who we're able to put our trust in. We have to hope for the best whenever we feel safe. We leave little hints of tragedy, as we try to open up our wounds entirely. We crave to have someone less judgmental listen to our stories, and it hurts like hell when we're able to let them in. The future is uncertain, and they may be gone within a second. It's something we all live with as we try to find our perfect fit.

She chased the world

Vibrant yet chaotic

She lacked confidence in carrying herself the way she always dreamt of. It was never easy to be free when she was shackled by the chains of history. Her pages had been torn to pieces, as she desperately clawed out of her tragedies. She was vibrant yet chaotic, even though she stood there silent.

She chased the world

Demons

She felt like escape was never an option, as she would surrender to her demons. They taunted her for years, as she tried to face her fears. It was all she ever knew in her moments within silence. They were disrupted by thoughts that would only leave her restless. She was trying, yet to her, it never felt enough, because all her dreams were dying.

She chased the world

To be real

She sank further into the blue, as the days would pass her by. She lived for moments yet nothing could replace the past that she would hide. Every place and picture had a story. They were a part of every chapter that she'd read before she slept. She found it hard to heal when she was struggling to be real.

She chased the world

Selfish

She lost her trust in friends and family. They were meant to be her saviour, or at least that's what they would tell her. They promised they would fix her, but they were living selfishly, because they never cared to hear her. They'd disregard her hurt, and hope she'd find brighter days instead. They never gave her space to grow, and some only ruined her more than what she felt.

Betrayed by blood

We're sometimes ruined by those that we call blood. We've only been attached by the way that we're brought up. We're family, yet the truth is that there are wolves among us. The worst feeling in the world is to be betrayed by someone you held close. They leave you questioning your worth, as you wonder why they hurt you with their actions and hateful words. We never allow ourselves to heal, do we? It's as if we're scarred for life when it comes to family. They're supposed to be the ones that we should love through every storm, but sometimes, we only make it worse.

You see, there's a time where you fall apart and your dreams shatter before your eyes. You thought you were somewhere safe, but suddenly, you end up in the cold. Your heart begins to bleed in blue, and you know why that is? You were made to believe that everyone you're related to is someone you should admire, when it's not entirely the truth. Some of them will hurt you. Some of them will sink their teeth into your skin and make you hate yourself within. It's a part of life, I guess. We rarely reconcile because we're not meant to make amends. It doesn't mean that we failed. We just never had a place for one another in the future.

She chased the world

Fragile eyes

She was blinded by her self-perception. She would never seem to view herself as fully as others did. She was brought up on nothing more than lies, as her worth had been stripped by those that she had loved. Was it ever love if they took away her pride? It was all she ever knew in the God forsaken sadness behind her fragile eyes.

She chased the world

Scars

She carried scars around her mind and her body, reminding her that life isn't always made of beauty. Her hands were tied behind her back, as she fell for liars that changed her mind entirely. They wanted to have control. They wanted to erase her angelic smile with their brutality.

Broken heart

She would always trust too much, hoping to find someone to heal her broken heart. She wanted nothing more than to be found, but the silence never gave her hope. She was on a never-ending search to heal the wounds left by hell on earth.

She chased the world

Venom and regret

She wrote stories across her chest laced with venom and regret. She fell for love in all its emptiness, yet little did she know that it was made to leave her breathless. She always felt alone. She always felt like something's missing, so she never had a home. It's as if she fell to pieces in a place where nothing ever stayed as it was before.

She chased the world

Behind the mask

She would suddenly detach from family and friends, wondering why she felt afraid to let them in. She was scared that they would see her behind the mask she's wearing. She wore it so beautifully, as if it were the skin that she'd been living in. It was all a part of loneliness. She never wanted the truth to find a witness, because she felt that no one would care to listen.

She chased the world

Fairy tales

She would run across the fields at night, staring at the stars that shined so bright. She loved the thought of escaping reality and what it did to her. She believed in fairy tales because her past was one trauma after another. It's what we do to make sense of why we're hurting. She just wanted to feel silence when her mind had only been chaotic.

She chased the world

She held the universe

She clutched the universe tightly in her hands, but it somehow slipped between her fingers. She lost touch of who she was, even though some would say she never truly knew at all. She was gifted with such grace yet stumbled when it came to bitter truths. She never wanted to feel threatened with the walls that she had built. She feared that they would crumble if she put her trust within another soul.

The cycle

She lacked the courage to be honest, and honestly, it felt like she was stuck inside a cycle. Her lips would only tremble, as she tried to keep them shut. They were sewn together tightly because she was scared to lose another friend. She didn't want to utter words that no one would believe. She had always felt insignificant wherever she would be. She'd only sit in silence to avoid the judging eyes around her. She couldn't bear to be surrounded when she was made to feel like she's a liar.

She chased the world

The wolves

There was a time where she could smile. She was genuinely happy in a world which she created, but the wolves took apart her innocence and left her with scars that never healed. She was torn apart by trust. She was reduced to tears by strangers who somehow look like us.

She chased the world

A touch of sadness

She felt a touch of sadness, as she felt a hand upon her. She never quite knew what was happening, but her purity was lost within a second. She feared to say a word. She felt like she was silenced. It changed her world entirely, and her skin became a problem. She felt insecure and dirty. She wanted to wash away the sin that was never hers to carry. She was so young and beautiful, yet life is cruel to even those who have their innocence.

She chased the world

Wronged

Her life had been a tragedy, but still, deep inside, she was full of beauty. She never saw it. She couldn't handle seeing herself as someone good, because bad things never happen to good people. That was what she made herself believe. She was tainted by the memories. She was left trying to erase what her eyes had seen, and her skin had felt. She wanted everything to disappear, but she knew she had others who relied on her. She was wronged, she was strong, but most importantly, she was brave enough to run when the world was far from where she's standing.

She chased the world

Afterthought

She believed that she's the one at fault. She would carry hate inside her, but only for herself. She hated to stare at her reflection in case she would remember how her dignity was taken. She was fragile in her time of caving, and the hardest truth to handle was that no one saw that she's in need of saving. They never wanted to admit that she had changed. They never wanted to believe that darkness exists within their isolated worlds.

Fallen angel

She wanted to remove the pain that she would hide, but she refused to keep herself on track, because she had a fear of falling down. She could never break the cycle, and it only seemed to worsen when she was stuck within the past. She had always felt as though she's grounded. There were times where she would try to fly into the skies, but her wings were stapled back. She was a fallen angel spiked with venom on her halo. The sad truth is, she couldn't stop pretending to be human, even for only just a second.

She chased the world

Hurts like hell

Some days it hurt like hell to be alone. She would try to scratch away the pain that was left sitting on her skin. She never felt like she could be herself again. She was too young to understand and too afraid to tell what's wrong. Her mind was full of sadness, yet she had to keep on running. It was the world. It never waits for anyone. She chased it without healing. It's what happens when we fight with time. If we stay still for too long, we're suddenly left behind. That's the problem. She was stuck somewhere far off in the distance, as the world kept moving on.

Predator in disguise

One day you may fall victim to a predator in disguise. They aim to creep into your life and hurt you by surprise. You'll feel as though you're safe, but you're not. You suddenly become immersed by words that they have said and the smile that greets you when they stare. You think the world of them because they hand you everything that you could want. The worst part about trust is when you're in a position to be manipulated. They break you down until they steal away your innocence. It happens. I'm sorry. The world is full of demons disguised as ordinary beings, but the truth hurts more than I could possibly convey. It's the sad reality of being human. You feel as though you're weak because you weren't able to say no, or strong enough to fend them off.

The truth is that you were taken advantage of by a wolf in sheep's clothing. You didn't deserve it, not even in the slightest. We forget that humanity plays a part in our demise. You may feel broken, but you're still human. You may hate the skin you live in, but you're still beautiful. I just wish that you could see it. The world is a frightful place, but moving on is about being strong, and I wish I could find the words to say, but sometimes words can never be enough. I want to tell you how it is rather than have you break apart without ever getting closure. I want you to know that life is beautiful yet twisted, and what you've been through is an obstacle that definitely affects you. I'm not devaluing the way you feel. I just hope you understand that life is more than bleeding blue.

You lose out on meaningful relationships because you're weary of those around you. You're scared of what could happen if you somehow trust again. It's a broken shade of beautiful that seems to hurt the most. You feel the eyes upon you, as you're trying your best to move, but are unsure of where to go. It's something on your mind that never seems to leave. You think about the future, and if your nights will still be sleepless. The truth is that you're a fighter. You fought the war of dishonesty, and I know it hurts to breathe, but you're still here. You should be proud of who you are, even if you carry all these dreaded scars.

You should have never been deceived, but sometimes, deception is covered in lies to make us sweet. My heart bleeds for you. It truly does. The way we treat each other is regrettable, but not everyone will hurt you. Some will lift you higher, but the burn will still remain from the hell that you have faced. I want you to know that if you feel discardable, you're not. You're amazing. You're the definition of survivor, and I hope you find the strength to push through all your demons, however much it hurts – however hard it is, from one stranger to another, I hope you find your happiness.

She chased the world

Burden

She was a cold heart in an empty space. She was made to feel like she's a burden, when in reality, she was worth the world and then some. She would always wonder why people left her side. She would always want them back, even if they deserved to stay away. It isn't easy being lied to. They made her believe that she was worthless. They made her feel disconnected, as she tried her best to stay apart from loneliness.

She chased the world

Keeping quiet

She wanted to believe that better days were coming, but her heart was unforgiving. She could never forgive herself for the insecurities that others left her with. She would always blame herself for keeping quiet. She would always hate herself for crying. She wanted to be real so badly, but no one dared to look beyond her tired eyes to see her clearly.

Ruined

She kept herself reserved, as she tried to find her place somewhere close to where she knows. The problem was that she never knew anywhere at all. She found it hard to picture herself smiling in a home that felt like nothing. She had no one. She was lost. She was alone. She was made to be the victim. She was made to only feel like she's been ruined.

Somewhere to belong

She wanted to belong. She wanted to erase the life that she's been given, but it's hard, you know? She would stare at crowds with her head up in the clouds. She would try to put herself beside them to see if she would fit. It's all she ever wanted. She was aching to be heard in a world where noise and static are covering the herd.

The sun and the moon

She knew that she could fight the empty feeling, but she had no confidence to do it by herself. Her thoughts were less appealing when the sun slept, and the moon rose. She was her own worst enemy at times. She would fill her head with regrets that never did her justice. She wanted to feel happy. She wanted to love herself, but her thoughts would only lead her back to nowhere. It was the light and the dark that brought out different sides of her.

She'd fall into a mess when the darkness covered her in stress. She was walking with closed eyes and a heavy heart, as she tried to face her thoughts until the sun would rise. You see, she was a damsel in distress, even in her fondest times. She would replace the guilt of happiness with her need to feel alive. She had to. It was how she coped with the death of time.

She chased the world

Death

Death was just around the corner but never came for her. She lost people who she loved, as the universe would take them before their time would come. It was another part of tragedy that made it hard to breathe. She had written every single chapter with one that ends in loss, but as she crawled out of her shell, there were those who gave her life. They were the lifeline that she needed in a world that felt like it was closing. She had few that she could trust, but the ones she would have died for were already dead and gone.

They were lost in memories that were locked away inside. She could never repeat the stories that they shared. It hurt too much to look back into the past, especially when all she needed was a friend. She would cry herself to sleep, wondering if they'll ever meet again.

She chased the world

Empty space

The death of a loved one is unforgettable. It leaves scars which never heal and fills us with regret. We wish to go back to what we had and whisper words that were left unsaid, but we know we never can. They leave an empty space beside us, as we miss their voice and presence. They're all we ever think of in our times of silence. We know that life can take as easily as it can give, but never understand why they had to be the one who's chosen. We're somehow lost without them, as we run through time, not wanting to replace the memories we hold dearly. We just want to say goodbye, because sometimes, we never get to tell them clearly.

She chased the world

Staring into heaven

She would stare out into heaven, trying to find a sign to stay persistent. She wanted to be guided through a life that was only stained with pain. She had lost the one who carried her through every storm but never could remain. She had lost her saving grace, and she felt the separation pierce into her veins.

She chased the world

Ghosts

She would break apart at times, as the memories of who she lost would suddenly creep into her mind. She missed their touch above all else, because their skin would make her feel like she was real. She had a problem with perception, and all she ever saw were ghosts from a time where she was happy. It was a part of her that she loved and hated, because even though she felt their presence, all she could do was stagger in their absence.

She chased the world

Left the world

They showed her a different side of humanity – one which gave her hope beyond what eyes could see. She was still imperfect through and through, but her imperfections made her beautiful. She almost felt like she was fine when they'd surround her with their energy. She felt connection in all its purity, but somehow, they left the world entirely.

Sanity

She struggled to keep her sanity as her thoughts painted scenes of tragedy. She was afraid to let go of what once was, so she tried her best to keep her memories intact. She would try to face the world alone but would crumble into pieces, because tears were all she ever had whenever she felt distant.

She chased the world

Always ticking

Time had always been against her. She never had much left to overcome the emptiness. She knew she couldn't stop, not even for a second. She wanted to believe that she could fight it, but time is unforgiving, as the clock is always ticking.

She chased the world

Meaningless desires

She would constantly play with fire, as she distracted herself with meaningless desires. She was afraid of life but found attraction to being reckless. She wanted to numb the thoughts that left her sleepless, but all she did was add on to the pain that she's been feeling.

She chased the world

Snakes

She hid her smile away, as she put her trust in snakes. She craved to be connected. She craved to have attention. She never realised they would be the reason why she'd be led to a place where she never felt like she existed. They never fed her soul the way that she had hoped.

Friendship

She thought friendship would be a path for her to finally find happiness, but little did she know that the world was getting further. She placed herself in places to avoid what she had felt. She threw herself into problems that were never hers at all. It was the only way she could stop the silence, or so she thought. She put importance on her friends, as she moved away from loneliness, but it only made her worse, because they never stayed the course.

She chased the world

Surrounded by lies

As the days would pass her by, her circle would suddenly decline. The faces she once knew had been lost in time, as she tried to surround herself with lies. She never cared for who she'd talk to, as long as they'd fix her life of solitude. She was tired of neglect. She was tired of bleeding blue. She just wanted to be noticed, even if it hurt.

She chased the world

Nothing in return

The strangers that she met took advantage of her kindness, as they gave nothing in return. She was there for comfort whenever they needed it. She knew how it felt to be defeated. She let them take whatever she could give, but in the end, they never wanted to be friends.

She chased the world

Two-faced

She never knew what was happening behind the scenes. They would mention her flaws when she was absent. They never knew what she had been through, nor did they care what she was feeling. They were only there to use her because they knew that she was giving.

She chased the world

Prying eyes

There were only a few who ever saw her, but she pushed them far away. She didn't want to be reminded of the tragedies she faced. It's what she did whenever she'd feel threatened. She would let go of prying eyes who may have given hope.

She chased the world

Damaged

She lost her trust in everyone. It made it hard to show herself entirely. She'd hide away her history, because she hated the chapters in her story. She didn't want to show that she'd been fighting. She feared the ones around her would only view her as someone damaged. She was covered in pretence, as she hid the secrets that she kept.

She chased the world

The silence

There had been a screaming in her head, repeating words that she once said. She would always call it silence because she never understood exactly what they meant. They had become part of her torment, and they were somehow getting stronger as she'd spend time with her 'friends'.

She chased the world

The thinning crowd

She had a habit of disconnecting, but to her, the days almost felt like nothing. She wondered why her crowd was thinning, as she let her presence fade. She grew tired of pretending, as she created space between herself and friends. She couldn't bear to face them when she felt like she was breaking.

The unheard

The problem with friendship is that it's sometimes built on taking. She was taken advantage of more than she could count. They stripped her bare down to the bones, as they made her lose her worth. She never felt enough, especially when she spoke. No one ever listened. Not truly. They never saw her for who she is – they only fed into her loneliness.

The beginning of the end

She was lost out there in the universe, trying to keep all of her friends. She knew that every beginning had an end, but every ending that she faced had been nothing less than tragic. She was holding on to hope that they'd be the ones to break the habit. She was begging to be saved in the company of demons, but to her, they were nothing less than perfect.

She chased the world

Self-belief

She would give herself to everyone. She had somehow lost her self-belief because of how the world had treated her. It was simply out of her control to view herself as worth it. She wanted to, but she couldn't. There were times where nothing gave her meaning, and in the dark, she'd sit, wondering why she's hurting.

She chased the world

Revisiting the past

The worst part of her had always been her mind. She one day refused to move with life. She had become familiar with the taste of emptiness, and it was fear that held her back. She never understood that no one can ever revisit what they held within the past – be it good or even bad.

She chased the world

Someone else's sin

She wanted to wash away the sin that controlled her deep within. It was never hers at all. It had always been another's burden, but she refused to see it. She viewed herself as the villain because she thought that she deserved it. She had lost what value she had left, as she frantically chased a dream of being happy without knowing what it meant.

She chased the world

Voiceless

She felt voiceless even when alone. She would whisper to herself that she'd be fine, but as the minutes passed, she would forget every single line. Her mind would only hurt her. She was programmed to feel like she was drowning, and no matter what she did, she could never find the surface.

She chased the world

Ripped apart by wolves

She would sit quietly with friends, wondering why they surrounded her at all. She thought it was for pity because she never saw her worth. It was hard to trust again when she was ripped apart by wolves.

A place within the world

She feared to trust a soul. They were only made to give her up. She would lose people as quickly as they came, and that was a breaking point that set her off. She shed more tears for others than herself. She thought she needed them to feel as though she had a place within the world. She could never be alone. She felt powerless and cold. She was scared the thoughts would give her hell.

She chased the world

Defenceless

The problem with trauma is that it leaves you defenceless. You feel as though you're strong, but the truth is somewhat different. You're never able to move on, because you fear to live at all. You build distractions in your head until you hit another wall, and suddenly the friends you've met become strangers like before.

Helpless

Her shades would never leave her side. They protected her from questions about her starry eyes. They were beautiful, you know? They sparkled with the tears that seemed to overflow. She hid away her sadness with 'I'm fine' or 'I'm just feeling restless'. No one ever knew the truth, and that's what made her helpless.

She chased the world

Validation

She tried her hand at love, but it felt so far away. She was searching for a saviour, but they only added cracks to a heart that never stood a chance. She gave herself to anyone that showed attention because she craved to find connection. It was a sad outcome related to what her past had caused. She needed validation to try to keep importance, even though she never felt it. She would still feel like she's a victim.

She chased the world

Another body

She had ideas that love would be her calling, but little did she know, she would be used as another body. It's humanity, isn't it? We go into things without a thought and suddenly we're brought to tears by the harsh truth we wanted to avoid. The lovers she would meet were only made to be a fling. She could never find her missing piece. They would only use her whenever they would drink. They refused to see her in her entirety. No one ever did. She could never be treated as a soul when all they craved was to get closer to her body.

She chased the world

What once was

There was a history of loss, and she never overcame the ache of what once was. She put herself in places that made her feel less worthy, trying to fit within the spaces of who she promised herself she'll be. It made her believe she could never hold the future. She barely tried to keep herself together, as she slipped into the places that always left her dark. She'd quietly remember the torture of being touched and the reasons why she never felt enough. She never had anyone to trust, and even when she felt as though she did, their friendship would somehow turn to dust.

She chased the world

Break

Some words were hard to say. They repeated in her head to a point where she would break. She lost the will to speak because she thought no one would ever listen. She wanted to share her story but the hurt inside her only seemed to worsen. She never felt respected, even when she was told that she should feel it. Human interaction had always felt so forced, and she never had the chance to open up to be herself. She was always trying to be somebody else, as her mask would change with the company she kept. She had many sides to show, but the worst was never on display, because it was the created from the memories she couldn't take.

She chased the world

Weightless wings

It's never easy to admit when you're falling. She would ponder why no one ever caught her. She was falling down from heaven with wings that somehow felt so weightless. She could never fly. She could never go back to where she used to be. It was life. It was hell. It was her story that she felt uncomfortable to tell.

She chased the world

Painted smile

Her smile was painted on her face. It was part of her that she somehow seemed to hate. She forced her lips in upward shapes, hoping her past would one day be erased. She never had the strength to make the pictures fade. They were spread out in her head like pages torn out by mistake. She never understood why life was made of pain. Was she cursed to be this way, or were there others who shared her kind of ache? You see, we never realise what happens to those around us. We give nothing in return as we judge each other based on our perception, but the truth is, all our smiles are painted to perfection.

She chased the world

Intertwine

We long to fall in love. We want someone to see us beyond the person we've become, because we're unable to show ourselves as clearly as we want. There are times where our stories intertwine, and we find ourselves immersed within another's life. We want to share each other's love until the end of time. We forget the damage that's been done, as we create a chapter that makes us feel alive. We want the world to see us hand in hand, forever screaming this was never part of what we planned. It's amazing, isn't it? We somehow fall in love during the moment we feel like we're giving up. The question is do we seek it, or does it come to us?

She chased the world

He gave her hope

She met him somewhere out there in the cold. He was unlike any other that she'd met before. He gave her hope. He gave her peace. He climbed around her walls, hoping she'd one day let him in. He saw a side of her that made him feel at ease, and he was obsessed with getting closer. He sensed her hesitation at the slightest brush against her skin. He would take his time to understand her, as their souls blended seamlessly together.

Stories of a life once lived

She wanted him to save her, but she couldn't bear to handle telling him the truth. She was scared that he would leave, but as the nights grew colder, she slowly fed him stories of a life that she once lived. He was the comfort that she needed when she felt misunderstood. He never judged her character, or the pain she felt inside her. She found solace in sharing memories of her younger years without spending nights alone in tears. She felt calm and free, knowing she had him to hold her through her frightful dreams. She was happy to be heard, even if repeating history only reminded her of hurt.

Building trust

She saw him as someone different – as someone she could trust. They were beautiful together. They were a chapter in her story that made her feel more human. He reminded her of warmth, when for so long, she had been running in the cold. She could never relate to the feelings that she had. She found it hard to accept that she found happiness. She clawed her way through life, expecting love to end in loss. She was surprised that he still stayed, and as time began to pass, she knew he would never go away.

She chased the world

Fight through storms

Love has a hold of us. It creates a belief that we can do better – that we can fight through storms in volatile weather. That's how it feels, doesn't it? We see brighter days ahead, as our hearts are slowly mended. We want to belong to one another, as we form to be imperfect. We can never find the perfect fit, but still, it feels amazing.

She chased the world

Safe

His touch was almost soothing. She felt safe within his arms, and the silence had somehow faded. Her heart had found a home, but still, she knew her pain was somewhere looming. She had never felt the closeness she desired, as she travelled through the cold without a hand to hold. She was begging to be connected, and in his breath was the oxygen she needed. She could finally breathe in a world which felt constricted.

She chased the world

Stories in her head

He would wipe away her tears whenever she'd remember tragedies of old. She had always been reserved, but she felt vulnerable enough to let him in. She had finally been able to repeat the stories in her head, even if they made her wish that she was dead. She found solace in his company, as he washed away her insecurities. He would reassure her that he'd help her fight the pain of yesterday. He wanted to be her new beginning. He loved every part of her, even in her times of tragedy.

She chased the world

City lights

They walked around the streets, sharing smiles and city lights beneath their feet. They were lost inside the moment, as darkness filled the air. They shared secrets and regrets underneath the starlit skies. They were so in sync at times, as if they were made to share their lives. They would treat the world as theirs, giving strangers little thought. They were the only focus in a world that lost its colour, as they created a place to call their own.

She chased the world

Just a dream

She was unsure if it was real, but she was glad that she had met him, however selfish it may be. She had never felt her heart beat as fast before. She kept him in her thoughts, as she replaced the tension of remorse. She wanted to let go of the memories that haunted her, even though many were filled with ghosts. She was in love with him. She was truly in love, and it scared her to fall this far, but she had hope that she'd be happy, even if it felt like just a dream.

Part of sadness

He was admirable at best. He was the reason why her heart was beating in her chest. He knew what she had been through. He knew the tragedies she faced. It takes a lot of courage to be part of someone's sadness, but he loved her and every flaw that she possessed. The truth about humanity is that we're flawed beyond what words could say.

The dates of surrender

She started to detach from everything around her, as the dates she feared were edging closer. She would attach her grief to days rather than leave it all behind. It's what we do without realising. We attach our past events to days, months, or even when the seasons change. It's as if our brains are wired to repeat the reasons why we feel like we're on fire.

She chased the world

Trapped

The truth is there's no way to save someone who feels trapped. He wanted to console her, but she only pushed away. She somehow saw him as someone else. It's the saddest story when it comes to love. She was creating space between them, not realising that things would one day change.

She chased the world

Loss of love

There comes a day when you both fade, and it's the hardest moment that you'll face. She pulled away so easily. She was stuck within a trance, reliving all her tragedies. The sad truth is that it made them lose whatever closeness they had left. He grew further from her at the close of every day. He never wanted it to happen, but sometimes people have to go their separate ways.

She chased the world

Cold embrace

She tried to stay calm, as she noticed the person that she loved had slowly disconnected. She was afraid another bitter ending was among her, and when she felt his cold embrace, her smile had disappeared from her sombre face again.

Obscurity

She had been through hell and back, but even then, she had to run from every fear she had. It was part of her destruction and why nothing would ever last. She genuinely wanted love to be her new beginning, but deep down, she knew she wasn't ready. It was another distraction to keep her happy, but what is happiness exactly? She repeatedly went through the thoughts inside her head, wondering why she felt so lonely. She had attached herself to love too quickly, and as her feelings went from positive to neutral, she relapsed into obscurity.

Falling out of love

Their love had turned to hatred, as the arguments became more constant. They used to hold the world together, but they became each other's burdens. They were both in pain yet wouldn't dare to say it. They were too lost as individuals to stay focused. It's what happens when we're falling out of love. We try our best to avoid each other, so we live our lives alone while we're a shadow of our former selves.

She chased the world

Neglected

The worst is always yet to come. She barely felt his energy. It had slowly been decreasing. His touch felt less appealing, as if he was too quick with every action. He felt forced to give her his attention. He stopped being persistent, and they both created distance. She couldn't understand it. She was worn down and made to feel neglected, but in her eyes, she had to stay to save them. She felt like she was worthless at the end of every day. She would try her best to please him, but he gave nothing in return. They had lost touch of what they used to be, but it hurt too much to leave.

She chased the world

'I love you'

The words 'I love you' were seldom said. They were a part of history that never made it to the end. She wanted to believe that fairy tales existed, but her heart was shattering to pieces. She felt him slip away, as she tried desperately to keep their love the same. She would search for what they had, but there was nothing left to save. She couldn't find the pieces that made her feel sublime. She would sometimes whisper in his ear, but he'd pretend he couldn't hear. Her words would fall upon deaf ears, and she felt neglected once again. She never thought that they'd be here, but nothing is ever clear.

She chased the world

Grown apart

She believed that everything would be better, but never realised that he was too far gone to be hers. He had somehow grown apart because he couldn't handle her at her worst. It happens sometimes. We rarely understand each other as well as we believe. We start to let go of what we have in situations that bring us to our knees.

She chased the world

The death of love

He would snap at every word. He was unsure of how to approach her anymore. You see, you can tell when love is dying. You can feel it in your bones. She lost the security in his arms. The warmth had somehow gone, and she slipped back into who she was before she ever met him. She would drown the thoughts of disappearing, but they were back to haunt her, as she continued with her grieving.

She chased the world

Someone else

He was tired of going nowhere, even though he promised to stay forever. He barely even noticed that she would cry when he was absent. He occupied himself with someone else. He knew that he was wrong, but the thrill was all he cared for. He would sneak away at night to numb his own regrets. He lied through his teeth, but never realised he would be a part of why she hurts.

She chased the world

Betrayal

Betrayal was never part of the chapter he had hoped. He detached himself entirely, and his eyes wandered somewhere else. He was afraid to break her heart, so he'd lie through a wicked smile. You see, in his eyes, he was protecting her. He knew that she would crumble if she ever found the truth.

Hiding deceit

He twisted words to keep her calm, as he hid deceit underneath his breath. He made her believe in every word he said, as he slowly watched her lose her mind. He wanted to be controlling, and it was her time that he would take. His manipulative ways were the reason why her heart would only ache. She needed to escape, but she thought their love would heal if all she does is wait.

She chased the world

Wolves among us

The memories were the only happiness she had. She would reminisce about the past, whenever she would get the chance. She wanted to recreate the moments that she missed, not realising that their love does not exist. She never wanted to let go. She was incapable of leaving. She stayed in places for too long, as she lingered with her love. She had never felt so clueless. She was slowly losing hope that their love was endless. The truth is, she was in love with a lie. He would leave her questioning her sanity, as he picked apart her mind. He was gaslighting her reality, as she quietly wept for not remembering whatever he would tell her. He would feed her lies to keep her satisfied, but in turn left her questioning her existence. She knew there was someone else, but he'd lie through his teeth to paint her as untrusting.

There are wolves among us, remember? They want to keep us around their finger as they make us lose our worth. We know that we deserve better, but through everything we've been through, we're scared to be alone. She didn't want to be fearful anymore. She didn't want the sun to rise and feel like she didn't want to open up her eyes. She had to find the will to say goodbye.

She chased the world

Another story

He left his phone laying on the bed, and her curiosity led her to the messages he'd sent. She found sweet lies he left for someone else instead. She was in disbelief of what she read, but had no tears to shed. She knew what the future held, and realised there was nothing left to fix. It was never in her head. He hid his true intentions until the bitter end and continued to cover his regret. She had to be strong. She built her courage up to let go of a love that had been dead and gone, but still, it hurt like hell to admit they'd be another story that she'd tell.

She chased the world

Back to loneliness

She knew loneliness too well. It always seemed to greet her whenever she was still. She would lay awake at night, phone in hand, and full of thoughts of what she's lost. She had to find a reason why her heart was bleeding. He was once the greatest part of her existence, even if they met their hateful ending.

Keeping love alive

Love puts us in a position to be lost within our thoughts, as we attach ourselves to someone else. We unknowingly lead ourselves to ruin. We place importance on the words our lovers spew as we neglect the bitter truth. We want to be happy. We want to have someone to hold us throughout our life within the cold. It's the warmth, isn't it? We become addicted to the feeling of connection. There are times where we have to stare love in the eyes and understand that distance disconnects us. It's the saddest situation to be in. You can feel the separation as it leaves you with unrest. You miss what you had before, and you know you won't have it anymore, yet you stay. You stay to keep your love alive. You're scared of what could happen if loneliness comes back into your life. It's natural. Life is about letting go and moving on, but we never find it easy. It's hard to breathe when we're reminded of our stories. We never feel enough when it comes to the end of love. We continue to fight with loneliness, as we wonder why everything we had is dead and gone.

She chased the world

Repairing what love did

She would fall into distractions, trying to repair the mess that love created. She was hoping she could focus on something other than a past that kept her seated. It felt like all the colours had been depleted and her happiness had faded.

She chased the world

Only one in colour

She wanted to escape from everything around her. It was hard to show her face, knowing her beloved had betrayed her. She was afraid that her life would end up going nowhere. It's what happens when we lose the only one in colour. We fall into the void, as we separate ourselves from what we had and back towards whatever we had known.

She chased the world

Disposable

Her confidence was shattered, as she wondered if she's worth it. She lost the only one who mattered, yet the sting of being replaced was what she mostly hated. She had always felt disposable, and in his betrayal, she was reminded of a past she kept a secret.

She chased the world

Tears full of memories

She carelessly neglected how she felt. She tried her best to avoid it because she knew she'd cry again. She was always full of tears. They carried memories within them that were always left unheard. They were her in her entirety, however much they hurt.

She chased the world

Beautiful yet flawed

She feared the world around her because it felt as though it's fading. She would close her eyes at night and the thoughts would fill her mind. They held her where she was, but the truth is, it was never hers at all. She was beautiful yet flawed, and I swear to God she was an angel, even though she was out there in the cold.

She chased the world

Life of misery

She lived a life of misery. It isn't hard to see. She would paint a smile upon her face yet knew happiness was somewhere out of reach. She ran, and she ran, but the world was never hers to grab. She badly craved to touch it, even for a second, but life had other plans.

She chased the world

Surrender to the night

The silence crept into her head, as she tried to fight with the strength that she had left. She thought about the end, and whether her time had come to throw it all away. She headed towards the window, and gazed over to the skies, as she wondered if she should surrender to the night.

She chased the world

A life to take

She locked herself away, contemplating whether her life was hers to take. She would stare blankly at her face, deciding whether life had any meaning. She was lost and so afraid. She had no one left to give her reasons to be saved.

She chased the world

Spiral into madness

Her mind had spiralled into madness, as she failed to chase a world that felt so heartless. She struggled to make sense of the life that she's been given. She hated everything about herself, from her soul to her skin. She felt as though the world had cut her breathing.

The canvas of life

There are times where we have nothing left at all. We never realise that life is what we make it. We create our own future, even if it's hard to be able to see ourselves as worthy. There's never a single option. We can stay in place or move across the open spaces. There will be times where we wonder why we're here and if we'll ever smile again. The truth is the past is over and the future isn't written. That's the beautiful thing about being an overthinker. You assess every outcome to paint the canvas you call life. We structure our worlds ourselves, as we write stories that are mixed with reality and hell. We'll forever be a broken shade of beautiful with tales that are hard for us to tell.

She chased the world

One to blame

She struggled to keep herself afloat. The loneliness inched closer, as her tears began to flow. The silence had consumed her during every single thought. She placed the blame on all her faults, not knowing she lost her innocence to those that she held close. She would put herself in places where others could be her saviour, but all of them had drifted.

She chased the world

Goodbye and a simple lullaby

Goodbye is all she ever knew in her life of solitude. She would hum a simple lullaby as she walked without a soul, or at least that's how she felt. She would stare at open places, wondering if she'll ever fit within the spaces. There was nothing she could do to make herself at ease. She was falling backwards in the streets, or so it felt. She wanted to believe that her story had stood still, but it hadn't. Time is a beautiful and hurtful concept. We may not move with the world, but we float like feathers in distress.

She chased the world

Running through time

She constantly ran through time, hoping to be fine. Her darkest days were all that crept into her mind. She was reminded of the faces she once knew, as she roamed around without a clue. Her history had been tainted by the loss of innocence, and as the world began to turn, the poison had been spreading. She fell too hard, too soon. Life had lost its magic. It was tragic.

Guilty

She would stay awake at night with a thousand thoughts that burnt her mind. They were from a different time. They were her in her entirety yet misplaced to make her feel as though she's guilty. She would wish upon the stars whenever they were present, not realising they only made her feel more distant.

She chased the world

Vacant

She was vacant at best in her times of loneliness. She thought about the past and why it always seemed to hurt. There's no escaping time or the tragedies we've met. She wished to find herself again. She was clawing at her eyes in hopes these visions would be gone, but they were all she ever had. She hated everything she knew because these scars had turned her heart to blue.

She chased the world

Dreams

She was tired and she was angry. She was restlessly chasing her imagination. The world would keep revolving, but she was always left behind. She would search for strength, but there was nothing there to find. She was drained completely from a life of tragedy. The truth is the future is never written until we fill our pages with stories we remember. The past is all we ever know, yet the present is where we're living. It's hard to separate ourselves from the ache of life and how we've felt. There comes a time when we have to learn to breathe, as we stop running after dreams.

She chased the world

Losing strength

She lost the will to run. The world was too far for her to reach. She had focused on the chase for so long and it hurt for her to stop. She believed that it would save her from the grief of what she's faced. It's all she ever wanted. She wanted to find acceptance in her isolated state.

She chased the world

Misdirection

Her troubles were all around her, from family to friends, and a love that was never what she desired. Her heart had been struck by ruin, and as she floated through the world in misdirection, she had felt like she was limited. She could never see herself as anything other than a burden. It had been her past endeavours that made her thoughts offensive. They belittled her to a point where her laughter was non-existent.

Paralysed

She was paralysed, not physically, but mentally. She compared herself to others, as she watched the world roll further. It was never her intention to let it escape her field of view, but when it gets too much, we sometimes fade into the blue. We feel our stories disconnect, as we try to start anew. It's a point of no return when it comes to life and what we've learnt. It's the tragedies of trauma that make it a concern. We're familiar with the taste of pain, but when the emptiness begins, we feel as though we're a shell of who we used to be.

She chased the world

Beyond the scars

She fought with thoughts that pierced into her skin. She wondered why her past had been obscene, and why no one had intervened. She needed someone to keep her calm when she was breaking, but all they ever did was give her reasons to be seething. The truth is, we always want to place the blame on others, and that's a reason why we stay within our misery. We never see ourselves entirely, or beyond the scars that keep us motionless. We fear to be misheard, as we step out of the silence. We push for change, but regress when nothing ever happens. It's a sad truth that's avoided because of how much it hurts to be reminded. We lead ourselves to nowhere, as we're torn down into pieces.

She chased the world

Fade

There will never be a time where something is meant to happen. We build upon the life that we've been given, but some of us will wait to see better days ahead. Truthfully, we shouldn't. We have to make reality our own, or eventually we'll fade. We become familiar with what we know and never seize the day. We always wish for change, but if we lack control, our lives will stay the same. You see, escape is all we crave, as we try to show the world we're brave. We fight off every single tear, as we stand still with every passing year. We promise tomorrow will be different, but as we start to age, we rarely turn the page.

She chased the world

Drowning

We attempt to salvage whatever's left rather than grow beyond the catastrophes we've met. We let depression overwhelm us, as we find ourselves gasping for the air that we've neglected. We never want to be surprised by suffocation, so we refuse to place ourselves out there in the open. It hurts, you know? We always search for hope, and when we never find it, we float around the surface until suddenly we're drowning.

She chased the world

Time

She saw that time was unforgiving. She aged gracefully, yet her mind was in a constant state of burning. She knew the outcome would always stay the same if she endlessly chased the world again. She wanted to regain the parts of herself she lost. She wanted to smile without the fear of losing what she's done. She knew that letting go would somehow be the start, and as she accepted what once was, she was able to see a different side of life.

Short of breath

She had attached herself to memories which left her short of breath. She never felt as though her life was hers. It had felt like she was living for someone else instead. It was the world she stood on which gave her nothing but distress. It had been the reason for unrest, as she moved across the universe. She would touch her face at times and wonder why she wasn't perfect. It was a flaw within her system. She thought the world was distant because her beauty had been fading.

She chased the world

Normality

She would hold herself at times and quietly surrender to her cries. She wanted to recover. She wanted to stare at her reflection and see beauty rather than disaster. She knew that she could conquer whatever fear there was, because deep down, she had enough of living when life was made of horror. You see, life is made to be unkind, and hers was nothing less than tragic. She was accustomed to being pushed down. It was a part of growing up. She found it to be normal. She found it to be daunting. She never knew that childhood would be haunting.

The last goodbye

She had distracted herself for too long. She went through every face and name, trying to stay strong. She would wonder where they are, and whether she ever crossed their minds. She would do it all the time. She would peer into their worlds to get a glimpse of whether she's still alive. She had always wanted to belong, but every bridge had suddenly been burnt. She rarely saw herself at all, because she tried to view herself the way that others did. She always searched for validation, because of a past that left her feeling worthless. She would put her trust in wolves, unknowingly letting them take advantage. It was a story that never seemed to go the way she wanted. She would put herself in places, hoping to be seen by snakes disguised as humans. The problem is that all of us are individuals, and even if we hurt one another, we all have valid reasons, however tragic it may seem. It doesn't mean that we should give ourselves away to everyone we meet, but sometimes, we have to say goodbye before they sink their teeth into our skin.

She chased the world

The end of what she knew

She fell down to her lowest as she pushed aside her love and hatred. She would spend her nights alone, scrutinising every detail of her story. She wanted to remove the pain of staying silent when her innocence was taken. She wanted to erase the times where she felt worthless in friendship and in love. She wanted to be a better person after losing those she cared for. She wanted to forget, but deep down she knew she would fall into regret. The thoughts rushed into her brain until she could no longer take the strain. She knew the end was coming, but sometimes, we love to stay. Her heart had slowed its beating and she could sense her vision fading. She was tired of being disrespected. She just wanted to stop the world entirely because she never felt like she could breathe. She wandered into thoughts of whatever used to be, as she closed her eyes one last time to fall asleep.

The saddest stories are told by those who smile, and she was no different. She laid there feeling lost and helpless, as she felt every touch upon her body. She felt everyone she's ever loved and lost, protecting her from the hurt that she'd endured. They were beautiful. She could feel them in their entirety, even though they had been in her mind and buried. She had never felt like she could smile, but as her story

She chased the world

unfolded through her thoughts, she realised that life was made of hurt and happiness. She found herself in her time of panic, and as the night turned into morning, she found the strength to wake again. It was never her time to leave the world behind. She finally saw that moments had transpired but they were gone within an instant. She was holding on to pain, not knowing that she was living in a different time and place. She was ruled by her emotions but never could control them. They were a part of history. They were the person she once was, but not the person that she is.

The truth is, she always wanted to move on, but sadly, she'd remember the reasons why the world had felt so wrong. She never allowed herself to be present. She let the moments last a lifetime and never had a chance to write tomorrow. It took some time to build her courage, but as she found her solid ground, she began to move more freely, and the world had become a fixture in her path to find herself completely. She never understood that people like her are meant to be celebrated for the pain that they've endured. She's a fighter through and through, and she should be proud that she still grew. She wouldn't be here if she didn't, and that's the honest truth.

She chased the world

About the author

Cyrus Ahmadnia, the mind behind the Instagram account @papikins is possibly your new favourite writer. Hopefully. Maybe. See you soon.

Cyrus Ahmadnia

Instagram – @papikins

Twitter – @papikinz

Website – www.papikins.com

Papikins

www.ingramcontent.com/pod-product-compliance
Lightning Source LLC
Chambersburg PA
CBHW071736080526
44588CB00013B/2054